TASTE THE WORLD!

WORLD
BOOK

www.worldbook.com

TABLE OF CONTENTS

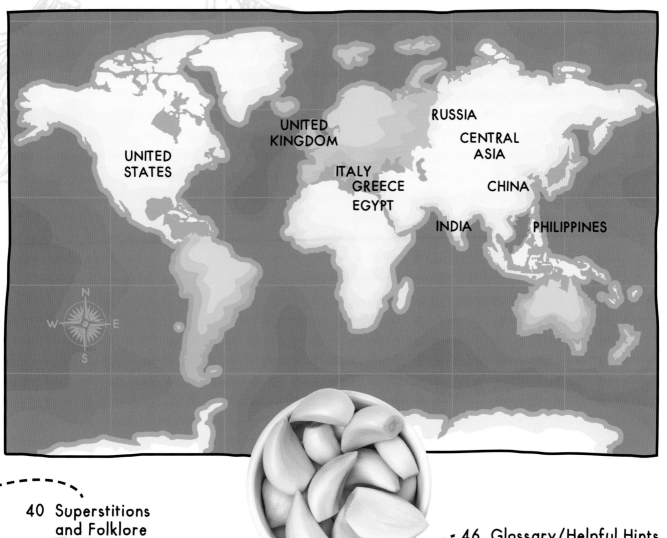

UNITED STATES

UNITED KINGDOM

ITALY
GREECE
EGYPT

RUSSIA

CENTRAL ASIA

CHINA

INDIA

PHILIPPINES

BEFORE YOU BEGIN

Included in this book are a few recipes that allow you to "taste the world!" Before you begin, look on page 46 for some helpful hints. Read the recipes carefully and always ask an adult to help—especially when handling knives or using the stove. Besides, cooking is easier and more fun when you work together!

ARE YOU HUNGRY FOR AN ADVENTURE IN FOOD? LET'S TAKE A TASTY TRIP AROUND THE WORLD TO LEARN ALL ABOUT ME . . .

We'll explore my history, discover some fun facts, and learn to prepare some delicious recipes along the way.

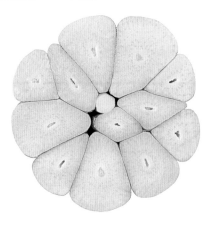

GARLIC!

As we travel around the world, you may read words that are new to you. If I can explain what a word means easily, I'll do it right where you are reading. If I use the word many times, or if the explanation is complicated, I will put the word in **boldface** (type that **looks like this**). Boldface words are defined in a glossary in the back of the book. For words that you may not have heard before or that are hard to pronounce, I will sound them out in the glossary as well, right after the word.

5

WHAT IS GARLIC?

Garlic is a plant grown for its sharp-tasting *bulb*. The bulb is the round part of the plant that grows underground. Garlic has a strong flavor and smell. Chefs love it because of its powerful flavor. Farmers love it because it's so easy to *cultivate* (grow).

Garlic has been used in cooking and medicine worldwide for thousands of years, as well as for religious purposes and superstition. Today, some people put garlic in almost everything they cook! Garlic can be used to add flavor and seasoning to foods that are baked, fried, roasted, or **sautéed.** It is also used in sauces, meat dishes, sausages, soups, salads, stir-fry dishes, and many other food preparations.

The word *garlic* originated with the Anglo-Saxons. It comes from *gar,* meaning "spear," and *lac,* meaning "plant." The name may refer to the spear shape of the leaves of the garlic plant. (Anglo-Saxons are members of the Germanic tribes that settled in what is now England in the A.D. 400's and 500's.)

I'm Dr. Garlic!

VEGGIE OR HERB?

Some people classify garlic as a vegetable. Others classify it as a powerful herb or spice. Some say it's neither a veggie nor an herb. But garlic is most often classified as both a vegetable and an herb. Garlic can be eaten raw (but not usually) like some vegetables. Or it can be used as a spice in raw or powdered form to season food or as a health supplement. Garlic is also used as an herb in many medicines to prevent and treat a number of illnesses.

A CLOSER LOOK AT THE GARLIC PLANT. . .

The garlic plant grows about 2 feet (0.61 meters) tall. The bulb has several parts called *cloves*. The cloves may be eaten or used for planting. A brittle, papery covering grows around each clove and around the whole bulb.

Garlic is easy to grow in almost any climate. It should be planted in late fall or early winter, about four to six weeks before the ground freezes.

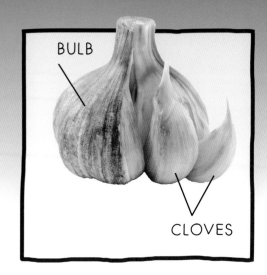

BULB

CLOVES

DRINK UP!

The garlic plant needs about nine months for its bulbs to grow to their full size, usually by summer. The bulbs may be sold whole, dried, or ground into powder. Garlic bulbs can even be juiced!

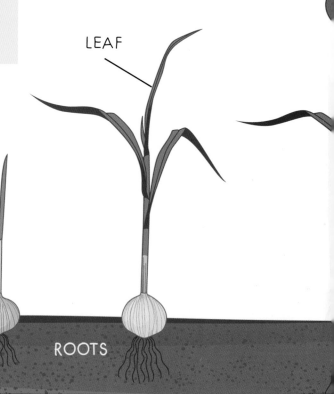

LEAF

CLOVE

BULB

ROOTS

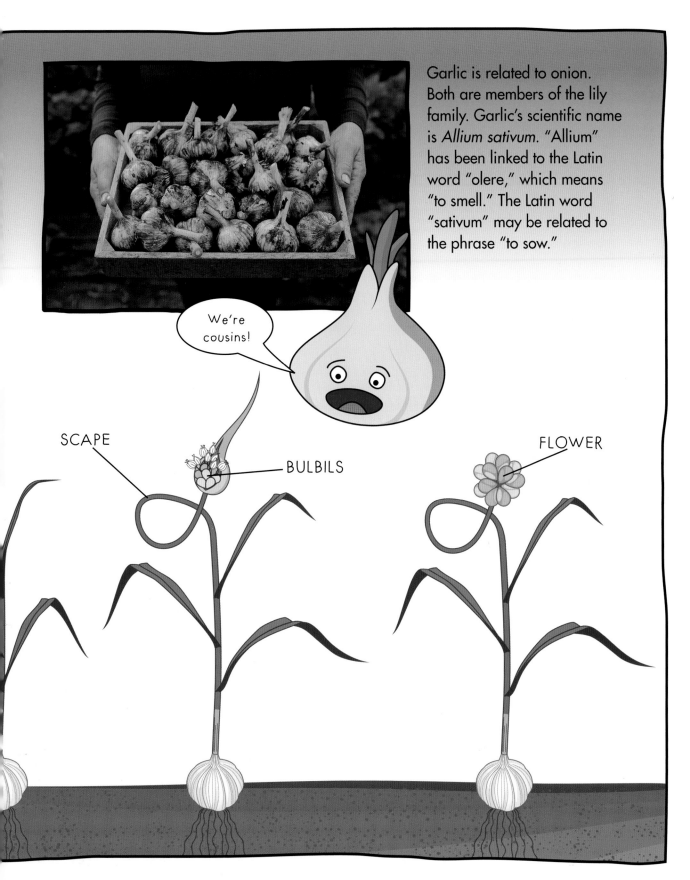

Garlic is related to onion. Both are members of the lily family. Garlic's scientific name is *Allium sativum*. "Allium" has been linked to the Latin word "olere," which means "to smell." The Latin word "sativum" may be related to the phrase "to sow."

We're cousins!

SCAPE

BULBILS

FLOWER

When the garlic plant sprouts in late spring, it produces a white or pink cluster of tiny "blooms" at the top of a long green curling stem called a *scape*. These starry balls of "flowers" can add beauty to any landscape.

Scapes are also delicious to eat! They can be put in salads or stir-fried.

SMELLY ROSE!

STINKING ROSE or pungent rose are nicknames for garlic. During ancient times, the Greeks called garlic *scorodon*. This was later translated to skaion radon, which means "rose puante" or "stinking rose."

Some people grow garlic just for the enjoyment of its flowers. But they are not really flowers. Garlic flowers are actually the **bulbils,** or seeds, that grow on the plant above ground. The bulbil holds more than 100 tiny cloves that are identical to the bulbs that grow in the ground.

KINDS OF GARLIC

There are hundreds of different varieties of garlic grown throughout the world. Garlic comes in different shapes, sizes, and colors. It differs in taste as well as the number of cloves per bulb. But garlic is generally split into the two most common types: softneck and hardneck.

Softneck garlic is the kind that most people eat. It is the type most often found in the produce section of grocery stores. Softneck garlic has a mild flavor and a soft, flexible, grass-like stalk. The stalk is easy to braid into attractive chains.

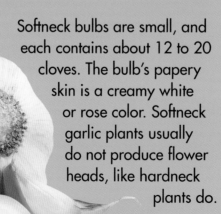

Softneck bulbs are small, and each contains about 12 to 20 cloves. The bulb's papery skin is a creamy white or rose color. Softneck garlic plants usually do not produce flower heads, like hardneck plants do.

So much tasty garlic!

Hardneck garlic does not have a flexible stalk, and it is impossible to braid. It comes in a variety of tastes and colors. It has a spicy, sweet, or pungent, flavor. In other words, it tastes more garlicky. Hardneck bulbs have fewer but bigger cloves, about 4 to 10 cloves. They also produce *scapes* or flower heads. Hardneck garlics can be white, red, brown, or purple in color.

GARRRLICIOUS!

Most people eat over 300 cloves of garlic a year! That is equal to about two pounds.

Bear's garlic, or wild garlic, is a plant that grows wild in damp woods, marshlands, at the edge of forests or by a river. It grows as a green-and-white ground cover with star-shaped flowers. You can usually smell bear's garlic before you see it!

Wild garlic is also known by several other names, including ramsons, buckrams, devil's garlic, wood garlic, field garlic, crow garlic, gypsy's onions, and stinking Jenny. The bulbs and glossy, green leaves of wild garlic are used in food and medicine throughout the world.

You can eat the whole wild garlic plant, even the flowers! It makes a good addition to salads, sauces, butter or cheese spreads, or mashed potatoes.

I come from a really big family!

ELEPHANT

REGULAR

GARLIC CLOVES

Elephant garlic is the largest garlic of all. The bulbs of elephant garlic can weigh as much as a pound or more! The bulb has about three to five purplish cloves, and cloves grow to 1 ½ inches in size.

Elephant garlic is also known as Russian garlic. It is not a true garlic. It looks like real garlic and has a mild garlic-like taste. But it is a type of **leek,** another vegetable related to the onion. Russian immigrants brought elephant garlic to North America in the 1900's.

CRUSH ME!

Garlic cloves hardly have any smell when whole. They release a strong aroma when they are cut or crushed.

15

IT ALL BEGAN IN
CENTRAL ASIA

Today's garlic grew from a variety of wild garlic found in central Asia more than 5,000 years ago. Garlic spread to the Middle East and northern Africa by 3000 B.C. via traders from India. Later, garlic spread to Europe.

HOLY GARLIC!

Garlic is mentioned in the Bible! During their journey out of Egypt, the Israelites recalled how they used to eat garlic, fish, and other foods when they were enslaved.

Garlic still grows wild in Asia and other areas.

Indian traders introduced garlic to the ancient Babylonians and Assyrians, who spread it to neighboring civilizations. Garlic is mentioned in historical records from ancient Egypt, Greece, Rome, India, and China.

Garlic has been an important crop since ancient times. Many varieties are cultivated and used for their tastes as well as healing benefits by people all over the world.

I'm bursting with goodness!

MOST OF THE WORLD'S GARLIC CROP IS PRODUCED IN
CHINA

The Chinese call garlic by several names, including *xiao suan, da suan, hu suan,* and *suan qing.*

China produces about 20 million tons of garlic a year. Other leading producers include Egypt, India, Russia, South Korea, and the United States.

GARLIC LOVE

Legend says that Chinese grooms once put garlic in their buttonholes to make sure they had a happy honeymoon.

The famous Chinese philosopher and teacher Confucius is said to have praised the goodness of garlic in his teachings. Confucius was born around 551 B.C.

DID YOU KNOW that Chinese writings first mentioned the health benefits of garlic some 4,000 years ago? Some writings suggest that the Chinese were cultivating and eating garlic long before that!

I'm very, very old, you know.

GARLIC SAUCE

Serves 3 or 4

INGREDIENTS

4 tbsp. (or ¼ cup) minced garlic
4 tbsp. (or ¼ cup) rice vinegar
1 tbsp. soy sauce
2 tbsp. granulated sugar

STEPS

1. Mix the garlic, rice vinegar, soy sauce, and sugar together and stir for about one minute.
2. Refrigerate the mixture for two hours.
3. Add sauce to any vegetable, fish, or meat dish and serve.

Garlic is a common ingredient in Chinese **cuisine,** including sauces and many vegetable, meat, and fish dishes such as black bean garlic sauce; shrimp, chicken, or beef in garlic sauce; and stir-fry dishes. Garlic is eaten raw, cooked, dried, pickled, or fried. Garlic cloves can be crushed, sliced, pounded, or used whole.

ANOTHER LEADING PRODUCER OF GARLIC IN THE WORLD IS

EGYPT

Garlic has been a part of Egypt's history since the great pyramids were built. The great pyramids at Giza were built as burial tombs for Egyptian pharaohs (kings) around 2500 B.C. That's some 4,500 years ago! The Egyptian name for garlic is *tomaya*.

Garlic was used as food and medicine in ancient Egypt. Garlic was fed to the laborers who built the pyramids for strength and endurance. This helped them to work harder and longer. Eating garlic also helped protect them from disease. They ate a diet of bread, garlic, and water!

I am so happy to get out of that tomb!

Garlic was considered sacred by the ancient Egyptians. Archaeologists (scientists who study ancient people) found garlic bulbs in clay pots scattered around the tomb of the Egyptian pharaoh Tutankhamun when it was discovered in the 1920's. Some of the pots in "King Tut's" tomb were even shaped like garlic bulbs!

GARLICKY HUMMUS

Serves about 4

INGREDIENTS

2 cups canned chickpeas, plus its liquid
½ cup tahini (sesame seed paste) and some of its oil
¼ cup olive oil, extra virgin
2 cloves garlic, peeled
juice from 1 lemon, more if needed
salt and freshly ground black pepper, to taste
2 tbsp. ground cumin or paprika (save one tbsp. for garnish)
chopped fresh parsley leaves for garnish

STEPS

1. Drain chickpeas and set liquid aside.
2. Put chickpeas, tahini, cumin or paprika, olive oil, garlic, and lemon juice in a food processor, add salt and pepper and begin to process; add chickpea liquid (or water) as needed to produce a smooth purée.
3. Taste and adjust seasoning, to taste. Add more salt, pepper, or lemon juice if desired. Drizzle with some olive oil and sprinkle with a bit of cumin or paprika and some parsley. Serve.

Garlic is widely used in Egyptian kitchens. Egyptian cooks use garlic in such traditional dishes as **hummus** and a soup called **molokhia,** in popular dishes including **falafel** and ful medames (mashed fava beans), and in such street foods as **koshari** and **shawarma.**

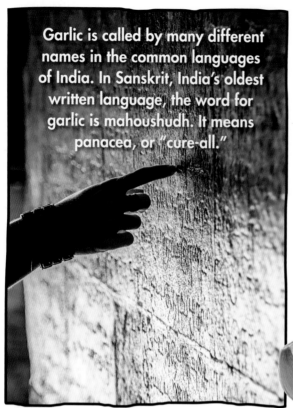

Garlic is called by many different names in the common languages of India. In Sanskrit, India's oldest written language, the word for garlic is mahoushudh. It means panacea, or "cure-all."

INDIA RANKS SECOND, BEHIND CHINA, AMONG THE WORLD'S BIGGEST PRODUCERS OF GARLIC.

INDIA

Garlic has been a part of Indian culture for thousands of years. In ancient India, people in the upper class stayed away from garlic because of its strong smell. They associated garlic with the common people. Today, garlic has taken on a near godlike status in Indian cuisine.

LET THE FESTIVAL BEGIN!

Garlic festivals were held in India during ancient times. Ancient Indian texts mention a festival where garlands of garlic were hung over windows and from rooftops and people wore garlic around their neck.

Come on, everyone, let's have a big celebration, just for me!

Garlic is popular in Indian foods, from **curries** and side dishes to street food. It is an important ingredient in home-cooked meals in India, after ginger and green chilies. Garlic is eaten raw, crushed, minced, pickled, roasted, fried, sliced, and puréed.

A popular Indian dish that uses garlic as an ingredient is *murgh makhani* (butter chicken). Just about all Indian restaurants in Western nations serve this delicious dish.

Another classic Indian dish that uses garlic is *chole* (chickpea curry). This dish is a favorite in northern India, and it is popular worldwide!

CHESNOK IS THE WORD FOR GARLIC IN
RUSSIA

The traditional Russian diet is hearty, and many foods are meaty and rich in garlic and onions. Raw garlic and onion are eaten with lunch and dinner, especially in salads. Raw garlic may be mashed and spread on top of bread, much the same way Americans eat butter with toast.

Pelmeni is the national dish of Russia. It is a dumpling stuffed with minced meat seasoned with garlic and other ingredients. Garlic is also included in such popular Russian recipes as *bef straganov* (beef stroganoff), *borscht* (beet soup), lamb **pilau,** and baked mushrooms.

The colorful domes of Russia's St. Basil's Cathedral in Moscow have a garlic or onion shape. The curved domes are featured in many churches throughout Russia.

PHILIPPINES

The Spanish brought along many elaborate garlic dishes. Garlic is called *bawang* or *tumpok* in Tagalog, the primary language of the Philippines.

Philippine cuisine is a mixture of American, Chinese, Malay, and Spanish dishes. Garlic is an important **condiment** in many Filipino dishes. One popular dish is *sinangag* (garlic rice). There is a saying in the Philippines, that a party is not a party without garlic rice!

Several varieties of garlic are grown in the Philippines. The Ilocos region on the island of Luzon is the country's biggest producer of garlic. Garlic is known as the "white gold" of the Ilocos.

HONORING GARLIC

The province of Pinili, Ilocos Norte, in the Philippines, is home to the Garlic Farmer's Monument. It was sculpted by the Filipino artist Raphael David. The Tourist Center in Pinili doubles as an educational garlic museum.

TRY THIS!

Adobo is the unofficial national dish of the Philippines. It is chicken or pork cooked in garlic, vinegar, soy sauce, bay leaves, and peppercorns.

DID YOU KNOW the Philippines imports most of its garlic? Locally grown garlic is smaller than the garlic imported from China. But many Filipinos prefer the native garlic because of its distinct aroma and unforgettable taste.

FILIPINO CHICKEN ADOBO

Serves 6 to 8

INGREDIENTS

5 lb. chicken thighs
4 cloves garlic, crushed
½ cup white vinegar

½ cup soy sauce
1 tsp. black peppercorns
3 bay leaves

STEPS

1. Combine all of the above ingredients in a large pot and cover. Put in refrigerator and let marinate (soak) for about 2 to 3 hours.
2. Remove chicken from refrigerator and bring to a boil over high heat. Turn the heat down and let the chicken simmer for about a half hour. Stir occasionally to keep from sticking.
3. Uncover the pot and simmer some more, about 20 minutes, until the sauce thickens and the chicken is cooked.
4. Remove from stove and serve while still hot. May serve over rice.

You can call me bawang, or you can call me tumpok, or you can call me garlic!

UNITED STATES

The United States ranks among the world's top garlic producers. Most U.S. garlic is grown in Gilroy, California. Oregon and Nevada are also major garlic producing states.

The United States exports millions of pounds of garlic a year, mostly to Canada and Mexico. But the United States also imports more garlic than any other nation! Most of it comes from China.

Garlic was brought to the United States during colonial times by European immigrants from Poland, Germany, and Italy. But Native Americans had long been using a kind of wild garlic that grew in the forests of North America.

Many people, especially the upper class, looked down on people who ate garlic. It was considered very poor taste to be caught with the offensive odor of garlic on your breath!

Garlic was not popular when it was first introduced to Americans in the 1700's. It was almost always used in foods prepared by working-class people. "Reeking of garlic" became an offensive expression aimed at Italian immigrants.

TRY THIS!

Americans love cooking with me!

GARLIC BAKED POTATOES

Serves 4

INGREDIENTS

4 clean medium potatoes
2 tbsp. olive oil
2 tsp. garlic salt (or as garlicky as you want it!)
black pepper

STEPS

1. Preheat oven to 375 °F (190 °C).
2. Put olive oil and one potato at a time in a plastic bag. Coat each potato with the olive oil by slightly squeezing the bag. (Or you can just rub the olive oil on the potato with your hand.)
3. Mix garlic salt and black pepper together on a plate for seasoning.
4. Remove each potato from the bag and coat it by rubbing the potato in the garlic salt and pepper seasoning.
5. Prick the potatoes with a fork a few times, then put them in the oven, directly on the rack.
6. Bake the potatoes for 1 hour or until they feel soft to the touch. Serve while hot.

GARLIC BREATH

Drinking lemon juice or eating a few slices of lemon can help get rid of "garlic breath."

In the 1920's, garlic use among Americans became more popular. By the 1940's, garlic had become a major ingredient in American cooking. Since the 1990's, garlic use in the United States has tripled. The average person consumes about two pounds of garlic a year.

GARLIC CAPITAL OF THE WORLD

Gilroy, California, is known as the "Garlic Capital of the World." The region produces most of the garlic grown in the United States. The smell of garlic engulfs the whole city. People say it's strongest on hot afternoons.

Images of the white garlic bulbs are everywhere in Gilroy! They are painted on the walls and windows of buildings. The word garlic is part of the names of many shops. Some shops sell plush garlic toys and garlic bobblehead toy characters. The city also has a garlic casino and garlic amusement park!

The Gilroy Garlic Festival has been officially certified by Guinness World Records as having the world's largest garlic festival! The three-day event is held each year in late July.

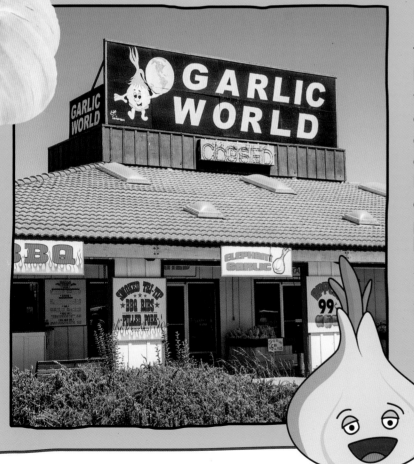

The Gilroy Garlic Festival began in 1979 as a way to celebrate the hometown crop. Many residents were embarrassed about the city's stinky garlic smell. But the first garlic festival attracted more than 15,000 people and made national headlines. According to *The Washington Post* newspaper, "Fame is nothing to sniff at in Gilroy."

A place to go and something to see!

The best part of the Gilroy Garlic Festival is Gourmet Alley. This is a giant outdoor kitchen where "pyro chefs" put on a spectacular flame-up show while making garlic dishes in huge iron skillets. Popular foods include garlic bread, zesty fried garlic calamari (squid), flaming garlic shrimp, garlic frog legs, garlic chocolate, and garlic fries. Since its beginning, the festival has sold delicious garlicky foods to millions of garlic lovers from around the world.

You can also find some vampire-friendly foods (without garlic) at the festival. You can hitch a ride to and from the festival on the "garlic train"! It is said that you can smell garlic in the air long before you get to the festival.

CHEESY GARLIC BREAD

INGREDIENTS

1 loaf French or Italian bread
2 tbsp. garlic powder
5 tsp. grated Parmesan cheese
1 stick soft butter or slightly melted
1 tsp. dried parsley

STEPS

1. Preheat oven to 375 °F (190 °C).
2. Mix butter, garlic powder, Parmesan cheese, and dried parsley in a bowl and set it aside.
3. Take the loaf of bread and slice it up, but keep the loaf in one piece. Slices should be about 1 inch thick. Spread the butter mixture on the top of each slice. Cover the loaf with aluminum foil, leaving an opening in the top.
4. Bake in oven for about 20 minutes. This should be enough time for the butter to melt and the bread to be toasted. Eat while it's still warm.

You're probably licking your lips already!

WORLD'S LONGEST GARLIC LOAF!

Etienne Thériault of Canada created the world's longest garlic bread. According to the Guinness World Records, the loaf measured 54 feet, 10 inches (16.71 meters) long!

DURING ANCIENT TIMES, GARLIC MADE ITS WAY TO

ITALY

Garlic was used during the Roman Empire as a food, a spice, and in medicine. In ancient Roman texts, Pliny the Elder wrote that the smell of garlic kept snakes and scorpions away!

It is said that garlic was fed to Roman gladiators and soldiers before battle to give them courage. The Romans also served garlic during lavish banquets.

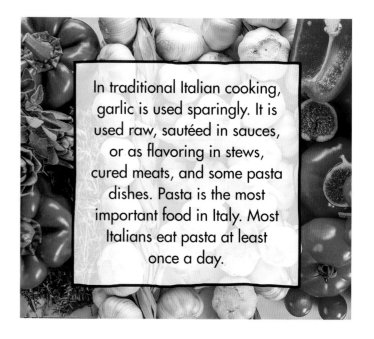

In traditional Italian cooking, garlic is used sparingly. It is used raw, sautéed in sauces, or as flavoring in stews, cured meats, and some pasta dishes. Pasta is the most important food in Italy. Most Italians eat pasta at least once a day.

NOT ITALIAN!

Garlic bread was invented by Americans. Bread is usually served plain in Italy.

DID YOU KNOW that during the 1700's, most Italians viewed garlic as a lower-class food? It was eaten mostly by poor people in northern Italy. Garlic eventually became a staple in Italian cooking, especially outside of Italy.

Italian cooks in southern Italy use garlic mostly to add a hint of flavor to pizza sauce and other dishes but not to overpower the taste. In the United States, however, Italian-American cuisine uses a lot of garlic!

A favorite dish in Italy is bruschetta. Bruschetta, pronounced *broo SHEH tuh,* is an **appetizer** made of toasted Italian bread rubbed with garlic. Variations of bruschetta are typically topped with tomatoes, as well as cheese, veggies, and cured meat.

"Buon appetito!" (That means "good appetite" in English.)

TRY THIS!

BRUSCHETTA

INGREDIENTS

1 loaf Italian (or French) bread, sliced and toasted
2 garlic cloves
½ cup extra virgin olive oil
¼ tsp. each salt and pepper

STEPS

1. Toast the bread in the oven or on a grill.
2. Peel the garlic clove and rub it on the toasted bread slices.
3. Season the bread with salt and pepper, to taste.
4. Drizzle bread with olive oil.
5. Serve while the bread is still hot.

GARLIC HAS BEEN USED SINCE ANCIENT TIMES IN

GREECE

Garlic was valuable to the ancient Greeks, who called the smelly bulb "rank rose." But people who had stinky breath from eating garlic were forbidden from entering the Greek temples. Archaeologists found well-preserved garlic bulbs around ancient Greek temples that date from about the 1800's B.C.

Greek athletes ate garlic to help their performance in sports during the first Olympics in ancient Greece. This could be the earliest instance of athletes using a "performance enhancing" substance in sports.

HERE COMES THE BRIDE!

Ancient Greek brides carried bouquets made with garlic and other herbs instead of flowers to ward off evil spirits!

Today, garlic is a popular ingredient in many Greek dishes. It is used along with onions and olive oil to add flavor to a variety of meats, seafood, and fresh vegetables. Classic garlic dips are a part of any Greek meal.

Some people love me, and some people hate me!

A popular Greek dip is tzatziki. It is made with yogurt, cucumbers, garlic, and fresh herbs. Tzatziki may be added to salads, used as a dip for chips or veggies, or served as a sauce on meats and fish. The most popular way to use tzatziki sauce is on gyros. A gyro is a Greek sandwich often made with pork or chicken (lamb or beef in the United States) and served with tomatoes and onions on pita bread.

Another popular Greek dip is skordalia, a garlicky mashed potato dip. This tangy dip uses lots of raw garlic. It can be served at room temperature or chilled.

IN 1548, GARLIC WAS
INTRODUCTION TO THE

UNITED KINGDOM

Today, garlic is a popular ingredient in British cooking. But garlic was not always an essential food or seasoning in British kitchens. In fact, cooking with garlic was unusual or seen as peculiar.

GARLIC IN WAR

During World War I, British soldiers reportedly put garlic on their wounds to kill bacteria (germs) and help them heal faster.

Despite its rising popularity, garlic is still a no-no for some people in the United Kingdom. England's Queen Elizabeth II is said to not be a fan of garlic. Palace chefs are forbidden to put garlic in any royal dinner preparations. This includes meals for the queen as well as the rest of the royal family.

Garlic flowers were grown in church courtyards in England for centuries. A wild variety still grows in the country's woodlands.

Do I look peculiar to you?

WORLD GARLIC EATING CONTEST

Eating garlic is a very big challenge in Dorset, England. The county in southwest England holds the annual World Garlic Eating Competition. A local farm provides all the garlic for this pungent contest. Contestants must eat as many raw cloves of garlic as they possibly can in five minutes.

The winner of the very first contest, held in 2013, still holds the world record. Oliver Farmer of the village of Charmouth in West Dorset ate 49 cloves! He beat out 25 other contestants, all reeking of garlic, of course!

WORLD RECORD!

Deepak Sharma Bajagain of Nepal holds the Guinness World Record for garlic consumption. He ate 34 cloves of garlic in one minute!

SUPERSTITIONS AND FOLKLORE

Garlic is often said to help ward off colds and cure warts, pimples, toothaches, and all kinds of ailments. Other folklore says garlic is also useful in warding off demons!

The ancient Egyptians used garlic in rituals. They believed that garlic could prolong life.

The ancient Greeks put garlic on stones at crossroads. The garlic was supposed to cause the evil spirits to lose their way. Another belief from folklore says that garlic hung over doors and windows, or carried in your pocket, keeps witches and werewolves away!

Garlic was used long ago as an ingredient in love potions to make someone fall in love with you!

According to superstition, dreaming of garlic brings good luck. Another says that if you put slices of garlic inside your shoes, it would cure whooping cough!

WHO'S AFRAID OF GARLIC!

Some people are really afraid of garlic. They have a **phobia,** or extreme fear, called **alliumphobia.** People who have alliumphobia may start to shake or have a hard time breathing when they're around garlic. They also may avoid onions and other plants with a strong odor.

Do vampires have alliumphobia?

The most famous superstition about garlic is that it keeps vampires away. A vampire is a dead person who supposedly rises at night to bite people and suck their blood as they sleep. According to legend, vampires hate the smell of garlic. So if you rub garlic on doorframes or wear a string of garlic bulbs around your neck, it might keep vampires from biting YOU and sucking YOUR blood!

HOW TO BUY GARLIC

1. Garlic bulbs should be completely dry and heavy.

2. Cloves should be firm, plump, and tight, not soft, spongy, or shriveled.

3. Choose bulbs that are covered in lots of papery skins.

4. Avoid cloves that have green shoots; they are no longer fresh.

5. Avoid garlic that is already minced; it has lost most of its flavor and health benefits.

Do I look plump enough?

STICKY STUFF!

You can make glue from the sticky juice in garlic cloves.

GROW YOUR OWN
GARLIC

Garlic is an excellent choice to grow in your own vegetable garden or backyard. Garlic is easy to grow in almost any climate. It doesn't take up a lot of space or need a lot of care. Plus, it tastes so good!

The first thing you need to do is decide which type of garlic you want to grow— softneck or hardneck—based on the climate where you live. Softnecks grow best in mild climates. Hardnecks grow better in a winter environment. Some people grow both types.

Fall is the best time to plant garlic. All you need is a sunny location and potting soil. If you're using a container, make sure it has drainage holes in the bottom.

CELEBRATE GARLIC!

April is National Garlic Month in the United States. April 19 is National Garlic Day.

A reason to celebrate!

Break apart the bulbs into individual cloves. Place each clove in a hole or trench about 6 inches apart in well-drained soil. The pointy side of the clove should be up. Cover the tips with soil. When the green shoots appear, put mulch around them. Cover them completely when frost starts to kill the young plants.

In the spring, pull the mulch back so the new plants can get sunlight. Water the plants about once a week, if the soil is dry.

The garlic is ready to be harvested by late June when the leaves start to die or turn yellow. Gently lift the bulbs out of the ground with a gardening trowel or fork. Place the bulbs in a warm, airy spot to dry for several days.

Once the bulbs have dried, it's time to store them. Clean off any dirt left on the bulbs and cut off or braid the leaves of the garlic plant. It's best to place bulbs on a metal rack or hang up the braids so that air can flow around them. The bulbs can be stored for three months or longer in a cool, dry place.

GLOSSARY

alliumphobia *(AL ee uhm FOH bee uh)* The fear of garlic.

appetizer *(AP uh TY zuhr)* The first part of a meal.

bulbil *(BUHL buhl)* An aerial bud with fleshy scales, taking the place of flowers, as in garlic.

condiment *(KON duh muhnt)* Something used to give flavor and relish to food.

cuisine *(kwih ZEEN)* A style of cooking or preparing food.

curry *(KUR ee)* A peppery sauce made from a mixture of spices, seeds, and turmeric. Curry is a popular seasoning in India.

falafel *(fuh LAH fuhl)* A Middle Eastern dish of spicy, deep-fried balls of mashed chickpeas or other legumes, served in pita bread with sauce.

hummus *(HUHM uhs)* A Middle Eastern appetizer; a thick spread or dip made from ground chickpeas, sesame oil, garlic, and parsley.

koshari *(KOH shah ree)* An Egyptian street food made of a layering of rice, macaroni, lentils, chickpeas, and garlic, and topped with fried onions and thick red sauce (sometimes chili sauce).

leek *(leek)* A vegetable somewhat like a long, thick, green onion.

molokhia *(moh loh HAY uh)* An Egyptian soup made from chopped mallow leaves mixed with ground coriander and garlic. Coriander is a strong-smelling herb related to parsley.

pilau *(pih LAW)* or **pilaf** *(pih LAHF)* Rice or cracked wheat boiled with mutton, fowl, or fish, and flavored with spices and raisins.

phobia *(FOH bee uh)* An irrational fear of a certain thing or group of things.

sauté *(soh TAY)* Cooked or browned in a little fat, usually quickly and over a hot fire.

shawarma *(shah WAHR muh)* A popular street food in Egypt; meat cooked on a spit and served in a wrap similar to the famous Greek gyros, but with an Egyptian twist—tahini (sesame seed paste) and tomaya (garlic sauce).

Thanks for coming along on our *Taste the World* travels!

HELPFUL HINTS

When working in the kitchen with food, keep these helpful hints in mind to make sure your work goes smoothly and safely. Then enjoy the tasty treats you make!

- **Wash your hands** before you begin food preparation and after you've touched raw eggs or meat.
- Thoroughly **wash fruits and vegetables.**
- **Use oven mitts** when handling hot pots, pans, or trays.
- **Have an adult help** when working with knives and hot stoves or ovens.

INDEX

World Book, Inc.
180 North LaSalle Street
Suite 900
Chicago, Illinois 60601
USA

For information about other "Taste the World!" titles, as well as other World Book print and digital publications, please go to www.worldbook.com.

For information about other World Book publications, call 1-800-WORLDBK (967-5325).

For information about sales to schools and libraries, call 1-800-975-3250 (United States) or 1-800-837-5365 (Canada).

Library of Congress Cataloging-in-Publication Data for this volume has been applied for.

Taste the World!
ISBN: 978-0-7166-2858-3 (set, hc.)

Garlic
ISBN: 978-0-7166-2861-3 (hc.)

Also available as:
ISBN: 978-0-7166-2869-9 (e-book)

Printed in China by RR Donnelley, Guangdong Province
1st printing July 2019

STAFF

Editorial

Writer
  Mellonee Carrigan

Manager, New Product
  Development
  Nick Kilzer

Proofreader
  Nathalie Strassheim

Manager, Contracts and
  Compliance
  (Rights and Permissions)
  Loranne K. Shields

Manager, Indexing Services
  David Pofelski

Digital

Director, Digital Product
  Development
  Erika Meller

Digital Product Manager
  Jonathan Wills

Graphics and Design

Coordinator, Design
  Development and Production
  Brenda Tropinski

Senior Visual
  Communications Designer
  Melanie Bender

Media Editor
  Rosalia Bledsoe

Senior Web Designer/Digital
  Media Developer
  Matt Carrington

Manufacturing/Production

Manufacturing Manager
  Anne Fritzinger

Production Specialist
  Curley Hunter

ACKNOWLEDGMENTS

Cover   © Fon Napath/Shutterstock; © New Africa/Shutterstock; Character artwork by Matthew Carrington
  2-3   © Shutterstock
  4-5   © Shana Novak, Getty Images; © Elen Vd, Shutterstock
  6-7   © Wuttichai Jantarak, Shutterstock; © Artem Kutsenko, Shutterstock; © Gunsan Gimbanjang, Shutterstock; © Dentan/Shutterstock; © Tim Ur, Shutterstock; © Elizabeth Salleebauer, Getty Images; © Seika Chujo, Shutterstock
  8-9   © Kazakova Maryia, Shutterstock; © Jiang Hongtan, Shutterstock; © Valeriya Tikhonova, Getty Images
10-25   © Shutterstock
26-27   © Tupungato/Shutterstock; © Alyona Naive Angel, Shutterstock; Alaric A. Yanos, PGIN-CMO Photo; © Leigh Anne Meeks, Shutterstock
28-29   © Gary Weathers, Getty Images; © Africa Studio/Shutterstock; © Quang Ho, Shutterstock; © Brand Kidz/Shutterstock; © Zapylaiev Kostiantyn, Shutterstock; © Vasily Menshov, Shutterstock
30-31   © Seven Maps 7/Shutterstock; © Danita Delimont/Getty Images; © Mariusz S. Jurgielewicz, Shutterstock; © Moving Moment/Shutterstock; © Jamie Pham, Alamy Images
32-33   © Robert Holmes, Getty Images; © Zahrah Zakaria, Shutterstock
34-35   © T Bradford/iStockphoto; © Oleg Voronische, Shutterstock; © Ildi Papp, Shutterstock; © Valentina Proskurina, Shutterstock
36-37   © Shutterstock
38-39   © Gary Blakeley, Shutterstock; © Hofhauser/Shutterstock; © Grey and/Shutterstock; © Dimitri Otis, Getty Images; © M. Unal Ozmen, Shutterstock
40-43   © Shutterstock
44-45   © SeDmi/Shutterstock; © Monty Rakusen, Getty Images; © Westend61/Getty Images; © Yuris/Shutterstock; © 54613/Shutterstock